Night Prayer (Compline)

in Traditional Language

C000057924

Church House Publishing

Published by   Church House Publishing
                    Church House
                    Great Smith Street
                    London SW1P 3NZ

Copyright ©   *The Archbishops' Council 2000*

                    First published 2000

                    0 7151 2032 8

Printed and bound by ArklePrint Ltd, Northampton
on 80 gsm Dutchman Ivory

Typeset in Gill Sans
by John Morgan and Shirley Thompson/Omnific
Designed by Derek Birdsall RDI

The material in this booklet is extracted from *Common Worship:
Services and Prayers for the Church of England*. It comprises:

¶   An Order for Night Prayer (Compline) in Traditional Language;
¶   Notes to Night Prayer (Compline).

For other material, page references to *Common Worship:
Services and Prayers for the Church of England* are supplied.

Pagination   This booklet has two sets of page numbers. The outer numbers
              are the booklet's own page numbers, while the inner numbers
              near the centre of most pages refer to the equivalent pages in
              Common Worship: Services and Prayers for the Church of England.

Contents

An Order for Night Prayer (Compline) in Traditional Language

Note

The ancient office of Compline derives its name from a Latin word meaning 'completion' (*completorium*). It is above all a service of quietness and reflection before rest at the end of the day. It is most effective when the ending is indeed an ending, without additions, conversation or noise. If there is an address, or business to be done, it should come first. If the service is in church, those present depart in silence; if at home, they go quietly to bed.

For further Notes, see page 11.

An Order for Night Prayer (Compline) in Traditional Language

Preparation

The Lord almighty grant us a quiet night and a perfect end.

All **Amen.**

[Brethren,] be sober, be vigilant; because your adversary the devil,
as a roaring lion, walketh about, seeking whom he may devour:
whom resist, steadfast in the faith.   *1 Peter 5.8, 9*

But thou, O Lord, have mercy upon us.

All **Thanks be to God.**

Our help is in the name of the Lord

All **who hath made heaven and earth.**

A period of silence for reflection on the past day may follow.

The following or other suitable words of penitence may be used

All **We confess to God almighty,
the Father, the Son and the Holy Ghost,
that we have sinned in thought, word and deed,
through our own grievous fault.
Wherefore we pray God to have mercy upon us.**

**Almighty God, have mercy upon us,
forgive us all our sins and deliver us from all evil,
confirm and strengthen us in all goodness,
and bring us to life everlasting;
through Jesus Christ our Lord.
Amen.**

A priest may say

May the almighty and merciful Lord
grant unto you pardon and remission of all your sins,
time for amendment of life,
and the grace and comfort of the Holy Spirit.

All **Amen.**

O God, make speed to save us.

All **O Lord, make haste to help us.**

Glory be to the Father, and to the Son,
and to the Holy Ghost;

All **as it was in the beginning, is now, and ever shall be,
world without end. Amen.**

Praise ye the Lord.

All **The Lord's name be praised.**

The following or another suitable hymn may be sung

Before the ending of the day,
Creator of the world we pray,
That with thy wonted favour thou
Wouldst be our guard and keeper now.

From all ill dreams defend our eyes,
From nightly fears and fantasies;
Tread underfoot our ghostly foe,
That no pollution we may know.

O Father, that we ask be done,
Through Jesus Christ, thine only Son;
Who, with the Holy Ghost and thee,
Doth live and reign eternally.

The Word of God

Psalmody

One or more of the following psalms may be used

Psalm 4

1   Hear me when I call, O God of my righteousness :
       thou hast set me at liberty when I was in trouble;
           have mercy upon me, and hearken unto my prayer.

2   O ye sons of men, how long will ye blaspheme mine honour :
       and have such pleasure in vanity, and seek after leasing?

3   Know this also, that the Lord hath chosen to himself
           the man that is godly :
       when I call upon the Lord, he will hear me.

4   Stand in awe, and sin not :
       commune with your own heart, and in your chamber, and be still.

5   Offer the sacrifice of righteousness :
       and put your trust in the Lord.

6   There be many that say :
       Who will shew us any good?

7   Lord, lift thou up :
       the light of thy countenance upon us.

8   Thou hast put gladness in my heart :
       since the time that their corn, and wine, and oil increased.

9   I will lay me down in peace, and take my rest :
       for it is thou, Lord, only, that makest me dwell in safety.

1   In thee, O Lord, have I put my trust :
    let me never be put to confusion, deliver me in thy righteousness.

2   Bow down thine ear to me :
    make haste to deliver me.

3   And be thou my strong rock, and house of defence :
    that thou mayest save me.

4   For thou art my strong rock, and my castle :
    be thou also my guide, and lead me for thy name's sake.

5   Draw me out of the net, that they have laid privily for me :
    for thou art my strength.

6   Into thy hands I commend my spirit :
    for thou hast redeemed me, O Lord, thou God of truth.

1   Whoso dwelleth under the defence of the Most High :
    shall abide under the shadow of the Almighty.

2   I will say unto the Lord, Thou art my hope, and my stronghold :
    my God, in him will I trust.

3   For he shall deliver thee from the snare of the hunter :
    and from the noisome pestilence.

4   He shall defend thee under his wings,
        and thou shalt be safe under his feathers :
    his faithfulness and truth shall be thy shield and buckler.

5   Thou shalt not be afraid for any terror by night :
    nor for the arrow that flieth by day;

6   For the pestilence that walketh in darkness :
    nor for the sickness that destroyeth in the noonday.

7   A thousand shall fall beside thee, and ten thousand at thy right hand :
    but it shall not come nigh thee.

8   Yea, with thine eyes shalt thou behold :
    and see the reward of the ungodly.

9   For thou, Lord, art my hope :
        thou hast set thine house of defence very high.

10   There shall no evil happen unto thee :
        neither shall any plague come nigh thy dwelling.

11   For he shall give his angels charge over thee :
        to keep thee in all thy ways.

12   They shall bear thee in their hands :
        that thou hurt not thy foot against a stone.

13   Thou shalt go upon the lion and adder :
        the young lion and the dragon shalt thou tread under thy feet.

14   Because he hath set his love upon me, therefore will I deliver him :
        I will set him up, because he hath known my name.

15   He shall call upon me, and I will hear him :
        yea, I am with him in trouble;
            I will deliver him, and bring him to honour.

16   With long life will I satisfy him :
        and shew him my salvation.

Psalm 134

1   Behold now, praise the Lord :
        all ye servants of the Lord;

2   Ye that by night stand in the house of the Lord :
        even in the courts of the house of our God.

3   Lift up your hands in the sanctuary :
        and praise the Lord.

4   The Lord that made heaven and earth :
        give thee blessing out of Sion.

At the end of the psalmody, the following is said or sung

Glory be to the Father, and to the Son :
and to the Holy Ghost;
as it was in the beginning, is now, and ever shall be :
world without end. Amen.

Scripture Reading

One of the following short lessons or another suitable passage is read

Thou, O Lord, art in the midst of us, and we are called by thy name; leave us not, O Lord our God.   *Jeremiah 14.9*

(or)

Come unto me, all ye that labour and are heavy laden, and I will give you rest. Take my yoke upon you, and learn of me; for I am meek and lowly in heart: and ye shall find rest unto your souls. For my yoke is easy, and my burden is light.   *Matthew 11.28-30*

(or)

Now the God of peace, that brought again from the dead our Lord Jesus, that great shepherd of the sheep, through the blood of the everlasting covenant, make you perfect in every good work to do his will, working in you that which is well-pleasing in his sight; through Jesus Christ, to whom be glory for ever and ever. Amen.

Hebrews 13.20,21

All   **Thanks be to God.**

The following responsory may be said

Into thy hands, O Lord, I commend my spirit.
All   **Into thy hands, O Lord, I commend my spirit.**
For thou hast redeemed me, O Lord, thou God of truth.
All   **I commend my spirit.**
Glory be to the Father, and to the Son, and to the Holy Ghost.
All   **Into thy hands, O Lord, I commend my spirit.**

Or, in Easter

Into thy hands, O Lord, I commend my spirit.
    Alleluia, alleluia.
All   **Into thy hands, O Lord, I commend my spirit.**
    Alleluia, alleluia.
For thou hast redeemed me, O Lord, thou God of truth.
All   **Alleluia, alleluia.**
Glory be to the Father, and to the Son, and to the Holy Ghost.
All   **Into thy hands, O Lord, I commend my spirit.**
    Alleluia, alleluia.

Keep me as the apple of an eye.

All **Hide me under the shadow of thy wings.**

The Nunc dimittis (The Song of Simeon) is said or sung

All **Preserve us, O Lord, while waking,**
      and guard us while sleeping,
      that awake we may watch with Christ,
      and asleep we may rest in peace.

1 Lord, now lettest thou thy servant depart in peace :
   according to thy word.

2 For mine eyes have seen :
   thy salvation;

3 Which thou hast prepared :
   before the face of all people;

4 To be a light to lighten the Gentiles :
   and to be the glory of thy people Israel.   *Luke 2.29-32*

Glory be to the Father, and to the Son :
and to the Holy Ghost;
as it was in the beginning, is now, and ever shall be :
world without end. Amen.

All **Preserve us, O Lord, while waking,**
      and guard us while sleeping,
      that awake we may watch with Christ,
      and asleep we may rest in peace.

Lord, have mercy upon us.
All **Christ, have mercy upon us.**
Lord, have mercy upon us.

All **Our Father, which art in heaven,**
hallowed be thy name;
thy kingdom come;
thy will be done,
in earth as it is in heaven.
Give us this day our daily bread.
And forgive us our trespasses,
as we forgive them that trespass against us.
And lead us not into temptation;
but deliver us from evil. Amen.

Blessed art thou, Lord God of our fathers:
All **to be praised and glorified above all for ever.**

Let us bless the Father, the Son, and the Holy Ghost:
All **let us praise him and magnify him for ever.**

Blessed art thou, O Lord, in the firmament of heaven:
All **to be praised and glorified above all for ever.**

The almighty and most merciful Lord guard us
and give us his blessing.
All **Amen.**

[Wilt thou not turn again and quicken us;
All **that thy people may rejoice in thee?**

O Lord, shew thy mercy upon us;
All **and grant us thy salvation.**

Vouchsafe, O Lord, to keep us this night without sin;
All **O Lord, have mercy upon us, have mercy upon us.**

O Lord, hear our prayer;
All **and let our cry come unto thee.**]

Let us pray.

One or more of the following Collects is said

Visit, we beseech thee, O Lord, this place,
and drive from it all the snares of the enemy;
let thy holy angels dwell herein to preserve us in peace;
and may thy blessing be upon us evermore;
through Jesus Christ our Lord.

All **Amen.**

Lighten our darkness, we beseech thee, O Lord;
and by thy great mercy defend us
    from all perils and dangers of this night;
for the love of thy only Son, our Saviour, Jesus Christ.

All **Amen.**

O Lord Jesus Christ, son of the living God,
who at this evening hour didst rest in the sepulchre,
and didst thereby sanctify the grave
to be a bed of hope to thy people:
make us so to abound in sorrow for our sins,
which were the cause of thy passion,
that when our bodies lie in the dust,
our souls may live with thee;
who livest and reignest with the Father and the Holy Ghost,
one God, world without end.

All **Amen.**

Look down, O Lord, from thy heavenly throne,
illuminate the darkness of this night with thy celestial brightness,
and from the sons of light banish the deeds of darkness;
through Jesus Christ our Lord.

All **Amen.**

Be present, O merciful God,
and protect us through the silent hours of this night,
so that we who are wearied
by the changes and chances of this fleeting world,
may repose upon thy eternal changelessness;
through Jesus Christ our Lord.

All **Amen.**

The Conclusion

We will lay us down in peace and take our rest.
All **For it is thou, Lord, only that makest us dwell in safety.**

Abide with us, O Lord,
All **for it is toward evening and the day is far spent.**

As the watchmen look for the morning,
All **so do we look for thee, O Christ.**

[Come with the dawning of the day
All **and make thyself known in the breaking of bread.**]

The Lord be with you
All **and with thy spirit.**

Let us bless the Lord.
All **Thanks be to God.**

The almighty and merciful Lord,
the Father, the Son and the Holy Ghost,
bless us and preserve us.
All **Amen.**

Notes

1   Psalms

If it is desired to use an unchanging pattern of psalmody for Night Prayer, the psalms printed in the text are used. However, verses from other psalms may be used instead, particularly if Night Prayer is said daily – Saturday: as set; Sunday: Psalm 104; Monday: Psalm 86; Tuesday: Psalm 143; Wednesday: Psalm 31; Thursday: Psalm 16; Friday: Psalm 139.

2   Thanksgiving

Night Prayer may begin with the Prayer of Thanksgiving from Evening Prayer (page 40 in *Common Worship: Services and Prayers for the Church of England*).

3   Gospel Reading

On suitable occasions, particularly Saturday night and before other festivals, the Gospel for the following day may be read before the Office.

4   Preparation

When the confession is being used, it may be replaced by another act of penitence. However, all that precedes 'O God, make speed to save us' may be omitted; this is particularly appropriate if Holy Communion has been celebrated in the evening.

5   Alleluia

The Alleluias included in the Easter form of the Responsory are for use from Easter Day until the Day of Pentecost, not at other times. The Alleluia following the opening versicles and responses is always used, except in Lent.

6   The Conclusion

The response in square brackets [ ] is normally used only if Holy Communion is to be celebrated the following morning.

7   Seasons

The hymn, the Scripture reading, the refrain to the Gospel Canticle, the Collect and the blessing may change seasonally and on Festivals.

For General Rules for Regulating Authorized Forms of Service, see Common Worship: Services and Prayers for the Church of England page 525.

Authorization

The service and notes in this booklet have been commended by the House of Bishops of the General Synod pursuant to Canon B 2 of the Canons of the Church of England and are published with the agreement of the House.

Under Canon B 4 it is open to each bishop to authorize, if he sees fit, the form of service to be used within his diocese. He may specify that the services shall be those commended by the House, or that a diocesan form of them shall be used. If the bishop gives no directions in this matter the priest remains free, subject to the terms of Canon B 5, to make use of the material as commended by the House.

Acknowledgements

The publisher gratefully acknowledges permission to reproduce copyright material in this book. Every effort has been made to trace and contact copyright holders. If there are any inadvertent omissions we apologize to those concerned and undertake to include suitable acknowledgements in all future editions.

Published sources include the following:

The Archbishops' Council of the Church of England: *The Prayer Book as Proposed in 1928;* which is copyright © The Archbishops' Council of the Church of England.

Cambridge University Press: Extracts from *The Book of Common Prayer*, the rights in which are vested in the Crown, are reproduced by permission of the Crown's Patentee, Cambridge University Press.